Fragile Cargo

by
Simon Jackson

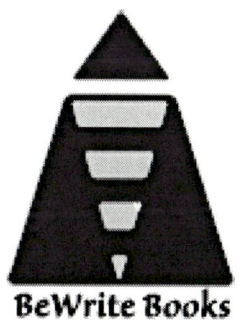

BeWrite Books

Published internationally by BeWrite Books, Canada.
208 – 19897, 56th Avenue, Langley, BC, V3A 3Y1.

Simon Jackson © 2012

ISBNs:
Paperback: 978-1-927086-80-3
EPUB: 978-1-927086-84-1
MOBI: 978-1-927086-85-8
PDF: 978-1-927086-86-5

Produced by BeWrite Books
www.bewrite.net

This book is sold subject to the condition that it shall not, by way of trade or otherwise, be lent, resold, hired out or otherwise circulated without the publisher's consent in any form other than this current form and without a similar condition being imposed upon a subsequent purchaser.

This book is a work of fiction. Any similarity between the characters and situations within its pages and places or persons, living or dead, is unintentional and co-incidental.

Cover design © Simon Jackson & Ali Hayes 2012
jakkojackson@hotmail.com
http://simon-jackson.weebly.com

Acknowledgements

Poetry in this collection has appeared in the following magazines:

Agenda, Ambit, brief (N.Z.), *Cyphers* (Ire), *Feile-Festa* (US), *The Journal*, *Poetry Nottingham*, *Poetry Salzburg Review* (Aus) and the Ragged Raven Anthology, *The World is Made of Glass*.

'The Ice Storm' won the Slipstream Encounters Competition.

'Defeating Gravity' was listed by *PK Publications* as one of the best published poems of 2011.

for Jana

Simon Jackson ran Living Arts Space Theatre Company for three years. He then became an itinerant musician, journalist and teacher in East Europe, North Africa and South America where he was Head of Drama at Newton College, Lima.

He writes poetry, plays, short stories and music, all of which have won awards. His short films have been screened by the BBC and internationally. None of this has ever come close to making him a living but goes a long way to alleviating boredom.

Born Manchester, Simon now lives in Edinburgh with his wife and daughter, who vainly hope he'll discover a taste for nine-to-five work soon.

Introduction

Much of Simon Jackson's creative work has been as playwright, film-maker, musician and short story writer, and all these elements mark out his poetry.

Many of these poems work as scenes and implied narratives. Some of them are clearly the work of a story-teller ('The man who saw too much' or 'Back to when the world made sense'). While a casual musicality lights up lines like 'Kelp lies piled like wet dogs' pelts'.

These poems take place in the world as we live (but do not necessarily know) it. Bars, hills, bus-journeys, bedrooms, classrooms and streets are their territory. Their underlying themes are those of our lives – love and loss, transience, joy, anger, humour, the inevitability of loss and the possibility of recovery.

I particularly like their unapologetic vulnerability, unprotected by smartness or irony. And I cannot but whole-heartedly approve a sensibility that writes of cows:

> *They know the end is coming.*
> *It is not despair makes them move that way,*
> *one slow joint slotting into the next...*

or in one of a number of tenderly-scrutinizing love poems offers:

> *I cling to you as if you were*
> *the last unperished life-jacket*
> *on this vast, empty ocean.'*

These poems are not concerned with displaying their credentials as poetry; they don't give themselves airs – they just deliver.

Andrew Greig

Contents

Introduction	8
Tiptoe	12
FRAGILE CARGO	13
Sex Ed	14
Schoolgirl Poetry Class	16
In Perspective	17
It starts from a spec...	18
Maned Three-toed Sloth	19
My Fever	20
Armada	21
Building a Box	22
Father's Chair	24
Homing Pigeons	28
Bathers	29
Casseopeia	30
Badminton	31
The Commissar's Reply	33
Frankenstein's Monster	34
Poppies	35
The Bride's Dream	36
Rapunzel	37
Satdae Neet Jazz	38
Smooth Crocodiles	40
The Morning After	42
Jacuzzi	43
Trapeze	45
Tiptoeing up the Mountain	46
Fragile Cargo	47

Awakening	48
Skin Diving	49
The Man Who Saw Too Much	50
Sgriob	53
Rendezvous	54
Prometheus	56
Fogbound	57
Ocean	58
Lifejacket	59
Mending	60
Back to When the World Made Sense	61
Ways of Undressing	63
Souvenir	64
Building Babel	66
Punchbag	67
The Ice Storm	68
How to Deliver a Baby	70
Still Life	71
The Naming	72
Defeating Gravity	73
Lost in the Forest	74
The Greatest Circus in the World	75
I don't give a fuck what you did on your gap year	76
Symbology	78
Cows	79
Panamericana	80
Reaping	82
Heritage	83
De Umbras Idarum	84

Tiptoe

A creeping mimicry of foetal position,
shrinking from contact with the earth,
shivering forward, poised for flight.

It implies dishonesty
to approach like a thief,
walking in a whisper.

This is how I offer myself to you,
deceitful, on tiptoe;
come to steal.

Fragile Cargo

Sex Ed

Male and female physiology.
Sexual reproduction in mammals.
Pre-natal development. Child birth.
I circle my hand
and enclose the uneven writing
in a chalk placenta.

"That is the scope of these lessons.
Anything outside this circle
will not be discussed."
And then, trying to hold back
a shiver of nerves:
"Any questions?"

Embarrassed silence, glowing cheeks,
eyes furtively flicking from rubber
to pencil to sharpener and back,
each endowed with symbolic significance.
Then one arm, extending erect:

"Sir, is it true what me sister told me?
She said that when her mate did it..."
and another arm, extending slowly as a snail's antler,
and another, gently waving until
the class is an opened sea anemone.

"I heard if you done it standing up..."
"Sir, why do people do it?"
"Does it go up the same hole a lady pees from?"
"Sir, does it hurt a lot?"

All these nervous, giggling, embarrassed faces,
each shining with eagerness to know
the secret rites of this arcane, adult world.

"Sir, do you and your wife, y'know,
do you and your wife still do it?"

When did our bodies cease to be
a solemn, magical mystery to each other,
become mundane, disorderly and vaguely embarrassing?
Once more I motion to the board.

"These questions are outside the circle."

Schoolgirl Poetry Class
(After Larkin)

They eff you up, your English teachers,
And they mean to, it's quite absurd,
Feeding you verse with such sordid vocab
You'd be straight to the Head if you used such words.

So the dangerous romance of Byron was lacking
In the balding trout of Hull Uni campus
But his ponderings on pill or diaphragm lent me
(Behind inch thick specs) a certain dampness.

The ritual woundings, tuberous cock and balls,
Had an effect some may think barking:
But between when sexual intercourse started
For him and for me, I was after Larkin.

The what has never but may yet come
Has a kinship with what wasn't and never can be,
There was no slide to happiness I rode upon
But I recognised the wish and desired it desperately.

I'd never trembling sat, but thought we could have
Shared joy 'neath Mr Bleaney's quilt,
Fantasised about fumbled tumbles,
Us both uncertain, not quite fulfilled.

Planned our reading habits, we'd mull over
Porn and poetry until half blind,
Dedicate me bitter, regretful love verse
In words not untrue, nor unkind.

In Perspective
(after Robert Graves)

'Get it in perspective,' she insists.
'At least you're still alive.'
Perspective. That old lie
that makes the wide rail track shrink
to a spec where she has gone,
that makes the circle of my glass' mouth
an oval egg from which is hatched relief,
that sets the parallel, true sides of our bed
crooked, the whole bedroom tipped askew,
that makes the whiskey bottle, from where I lie,
tower high above me as a church spire.
Perspective. The twisted fib
that by showing us the world as it is not
allows us to survive in it.

It starts from a spec...
(after Sylvia Plath)

It starts from a spec
a tiny dark spot
like a drop of blood
or a fly crawling down the wall
the head of a zip
travelling along a seam
opening invisible teeth
that will spread, spread wide
to open a new world
to engulf me
in its dark velvet throat
and leave nothing
nothing the same again.

Maned Three-toed Sloth
Painted from a preserved specimen for the collection of Cassiano dal Posso

Stood upright, on all fours,
the long forelimbs make it appear
a relative of ape or monkey,
it's small-nosed head of human proportion,
suggesting a man inside a bear suit.

Yet the limbs, straight as tree trunks,
have not the strength to hold the barrel body,
and the three curled claws, gun barrel grey,
were never made to walk this earth,
as impractical footwear as stilettos.

But who could have taken the derision
of trying to paint a mammal inverted.
Far more ridiculous than kraken or dragon,
a leap of faith as insane as the claim
that earth could spin around the sun.

My Fever
(for Jana)

Confined to bed, sheets sticking
like shrink wrap to my fevered skin.
The sun seeps through the curtains like a stain.

The sweet sharpness of peppers, hung in chains outside
to make *ajvar*, or *kiseli paprika*
and keep us the whole winter, fills the room.

Mushrooms are drying on the straw
and my mother's voice rises from the thick walled kitchen
as she stirs the chicken soup to nurse me to health.

I know you're dead. I know this country
doesn't even exist anymore,
yet the smell of fresh linen and *rakija*

rubbed onto my boyish breast
enwraps me more convincingly
than this new land or duvet that weigh upon me now.

Baba putting wet oats in my socks
to take away the fever,
mother scolding her home-spun remedies.

I feel my mother's hand, warm and dry,
passing across my fevered forehead
and know that all will be well.

Armada

No damp sand to sculpt into castles or schooners,
only stones the size of fists,
treacherous, deceptive,
ready to twist the unwary ankle.
She wouldn't have walked far this way.

Grey sky is pooled in cupped nooks in the rocks
bare of knuckled crabs, the quick shadows of tiddlers.
They clasp only smudged grey cloud
on their crenulated surface.
Nothing to hold a child for long.

The sea is cobbled granite
patched with a scrim of white plaster.
The tarpaulin hem of coast
is folded onto the shore.
Kelp lies piled like wet dogs' pelts.

An armada of rocky islets slice the surface.
She wouldn't swim so far.
Could a child be plucked unwilling by the tide,
dragged out, buoyed up by a pink M&S caghoul,
snagged by rocky fingers?

Could a girl cling unobserved to the blind side
until sucked away by greedy waves?
The wind on the headland steals my ever wilder cries,
snatches the child's name from my lips.
She would not have come so far.

Building a Box

He planes the maple in long smooth sweeps
of his joiner's hands.

Shavings rise like smoke
and tumble in a wave-break
of scattered curls below,
crisp and delicate as shells.

In my hands they are
warring scorpions, drifting leaves,
a cascading avalanche.

I am shooed away with hands
huge as oak trees.

The sky is wooden.
Clouds curl in whorls of grain
around a knot of sun.

He carves hidden joints and panels with
chiselled thumbs,
fingers blunt as hammers.

He pieces together
a box perhaps
a mastless boat. It seems
a simple puzzle for such hours of sweat;
his face is gleaming, head bent.

Slow hands build wood dark with wax,
sail the surface in tiny circles
concealing deeper maps of grain.

He will not come and join me
on the big stone table from where I
set sail to distant lands

or let me ride the tempest
of his hurricane shoulders
about the yard.

I watch. Waiting.

He takes me
shell like
to his warm ship of body
and sorrow breaks
over him like a wave.

It seems a small vessel to hold six
months of baby sister.

Father's Chair

I.
Behind the farmhouse lay a patch of hand tilled ground,
a furrowed rug between carpets of weeds
and rusting bones of broken machinery.
I shovel soft earth with numb fingers.

II.
It was here he sat when Nathan left,
all knuckles and knees and calloused dirt,
darker hide than the time stained oak,
a creature carved of earth and wood,
unmovable knot of bitterness.
The chair rocked of its own volition.

It was here he sat when Mother left;
the chair became as wind –
howling, moaning, shaking his bones
till joints cracked and threatened to sever,
yet still he clung to trembling arms
as shipwrecked man to last splintered spar
of his vessel, knowing it too little
to hold him afloat for long.
The chair shook crevices into his face,
twisted cruelty into his mouth.

Here I stood, face to window,
beating on impervious glass
as he emptied Bess with heavy strokes,
continuing till the only movement
was falling birch and shaking glass.

III.
I raised the carcass that held none of Bess –
only the smell remained –

and carried her against my chest
still warm and salivating.
Rain and wind blew peaks and valleys into her fur
while rivers of warm salt
threaded down my face and arms.

The hills howled a lament around
the black stone farmhouse
torn from the groaning mountain's side.

Behind the farmhouse I knelt
cursing man who raised me
and the hills and rain that reared him –
thunderous anger, hands of hillsides.

IV.
The earth - soft, black, heavy –
grew around my shovelling hands
till fingers were broader than my father's.
I hated him with rain and thunder
and all the emptiness beyond it
but knew I would surrender hate
when he softened with tears, bruised torn knees,
became the child and me the father
as after a numbing, undeserved beating,
seeking redemption from the martyred son.

I knead wet soil, shifting pebble and peat
and silver bulbs he buries yearly
to sink and rot, without real hopeo
of them ever seeking day again.

V.
Tendrils of root cling to fistfuls of dirt,
tenacious in their losing battle,
knowing the failed crops of the years before
will someday feed them into bloom and decay.

Father's shadow moves miles above me,
stacking stone in endless penance;
he feeds the mountain's unearthed roots.

VI.
The freezing rain is a part of me;
my hands are an ice age,
calving the soil, the stone, the sand.
They do not recognise the misplaced depths
of softer soil, the rotting cloth,
the stronger strands of sun fed root
that rise to air between my fingers,
the richer clay which will not move –
until thin chain enwraps my hand;
through earthy depths, silver glints.

VII.
I could not stop.

I claw around dead clay,
burrowing through skin and soil –
in my blood, beneath my skin,
and under my fingernails
she is part of me.

I could not stop.

Till ragged fingers, blunted with blood,
hold soft grey tatters to the matching sky,
cullendered with irregular holes.

I have never seen her in this dress
but know it like my reflected self
from the framed, starched figures
beside his bed.

VIII.
 I replace the locket around Mother's neck
and hate my aching arms
that they are living and hers dead,
that despite their life, can not raise her body
towards the sun she loved.

I will not look into her face;
I see it bronzed as bracken, glowing,
the only sunlight in our home –
to look at that worm encircled head
will turn my heart to stone.

IX.
I have no emotions, only the rain.

I cover my treasure.
I walk indoors.
I break the gun cabinet lock.
Silver glints in my lap.

I sit in father's chair and wait.

Homing Pigeons

I kept racers as a bairn,
I'd feed them cornflakes,
take them water in Ma's best china bowls.
She'd scold me like crazy,
call me a numpty brained heathen and threaten
that God hates a wastrel and would damn my soul.

I shrugged it off. I knew better.
I'd never see creatures closer to angels than these.
They'd flutter their white wings around me,
their calming song, a hush
hung between breathing and purring,
came to appease my most violent thoughts.

Da gave me the first as a wee one,
put up the cote on the roof of our block
and I built the flock up with aniseed balls.
The birds go mad for the smell.
I'd crush them and dredge the sweet dust
over the tails of my best fliers.

They'd return with a straggle skeeting behind
like a priest leading his flock
and I'd fuss and befriend them
and not let them out till they realised
they'd not ever find a home braw as this
without me to feed and to tend them.

It's daft, but I thought if I kept it like new
one day maybe Da would find his way home too.

Bathers

Sliding, silent as adders,
up to the lip of the dune
we stared, suppressing jubilant sniggers,
at the two nude bathers below,
flat out on the sand's hollowed stomach,
sisters we presumed;

we consumed their white and tan curves,
the bikini lines rising like angel wings
from each shadowed groin,
the halos in kelp and straw
around each freckled face,

until one's hand, slow and deliberate
as the calm sea's lapping advance,
caressed her partner's thigh, and I
withdrew, ashamed, though unsure why,
as at walking in unnoticed
on your parents making love
in the early afternoon.

Casseopeia

I stare at the dots of light,
blurred by tears,
try to find the familiar shapes
of the bear, Orion, the seven sisters.

There is no sense to these bright smudges,
no magic, no artistry, just windows and cars.
I rub my eyes and curse the city
too bright to see the stars.

I wish I was back home
where the black night enwraps you like a warm blanket
and each lamp has a familiar glow
and the knowledge of the hand that lit it.

Badminton

On summer holidays we would play
badminton on granny's porch
late into the hot nights,
cousin Rhiannon and me.

That first shot was always hardest,
fumbling with the stiff white skirt,
then sending it skyward
at some awkward tangent.

This was where I lost
most of our shuttlecocks
to the thorny bushes below,
game over before it had really begun,

but once we got into the rhythm of it,
it all seemed pretty natural: parry, return,
the white cone rising and falling
almost in time with our breathing.

You'd grown since last year.
The down on your forearms
was golden in the lamp light,
your white shirt clung tightly

to new budding curves.
I was mesmerised
by the perspiration
that glittered above your lip.

Nothing was as it had been.
Your skirt billowed up tanned thighs
as you leaped for every shot
and moths fluttered round my glowing heart.

You were transformed
from my ungainly cousin
to something inexplicable.
You got bored and went inside

but I can still picture the shuttlecock
falling through the black sky
like a sudden angel,
or a slow twisting summer snowflake,

the common-place revealed
as completely extraordinary.

The Commissar's Reply

Child with your scalpel eyes
that want to cut through thick wrapped veils
Child with your spider fingers
that would crawl into every chink
Child with your acrobat tongue
that would untie the knots that bind us deep

Take care – they are not question marks
at the end of every sentence hung
but upturned fish hooks to gouge your cheeks
and drag you screaming from your sleep

Frankenstein's Monster

Emotions, slow-forming as cumuli nimbus,
disperse within his aquarium skull;
each unnamed feeling, each hurt,
ingenuously drifting over
the rippling lake of his face.

A dapper, funeral clothed man,
deftly stitching a tapestry of flesh;
the convulsing pain of fiery birth;
a forced exile from the fear
and anger of hind-legged creatures.

All this seemed far away;
the warmth of the sun, the smell of meadow,
and the cool grasp of flowing water were good.

Poppies

A single heartbeat impossibly amplified,
a crash like thunder
and you buckle by my side,
suddenly limp as crumpled orders.

A red flower blooms through your khaki jacket
in its centre a black hole, a full stop,
as unexpected as a single poppy
growing wild in a field of crops.

It is the inside of a gaping thrush's beak
shrieking its life wish, its need, its hunger,
a flame consuming everything,
the scream of an open mouth in anger,

the red gash between spread thighs,
an entrance forced by this invasion,
borders and boundaries violently breached,
starting an unstoppable migration.

The Bride's Dream

The sheet and blanket loll from the mattress' palette,
the pillow a sneering upper lip.
The bed will devour me, she thinks,
the linen is stained, the colour of old teeth.

He throws aside shirt and jacket, unsheathing himself,
eager to sacrifice us. He beckons.
The piebald carpet digests my footsteps.
The bed makes no sound as I sink in.

Heedless of bruising ripe flesh
he unpeels me like fruit.
Puddled beneath him, a saliva shadow,
I sink into the bed like juice.

Rapunzel

Once upon a time she heard
a voice calling her true name
in a way no-one had called before,
it resonated in her breast
as an aching echo.
The cathedral of her rib cage
sang to his voice as a glass
to the caress of a licked finger.
His closeness lit a slow heat
there, between her thighs, a pressure
like wood turning on wood, threatening
to leap into improbable flame.

So she let down her hair and he clambered up,
hand over hand, clutching, grasping,
grunting at her. The pain was terrible
but finally he was in
and it all seemed worth it for a time.

And now here he is, in her small chamber,
bigger and harder to hide each day.
Christ, she never meant him to stay!
It was far too late to ask him politely
to pack his things and leave.
In the end she cut him out with a knife.

The next time she heard that call
to let her hair hang down
she leaned out of the tower block,
shook her head into the wind's caresses
letting everybody see her newly crew-cut tresses.

Satdae Neet Jazz

The finger jabs a gnarly beat
his body bended layk a drummers
oer our table, but ahm no listenin

cos the lassie across the bar is croonin
a sultry tune fer me alone.
She clocks mah eye an the looks electric

she shimmers in its spot light.
She raises the Smirnoff Ice mic
an parts her lips tae sing tae me.

Flash o ivory white teeth,
tongue dartin oer them layk a digit
ticklin a tune frae piana keys,

every bit as delibrate, precise,
she tosses back her head an stabs
a trumpet riff o laughter oot

her hair a glistenin glissando
playin tae the stalls but aimin
tae this wan spectator in the gods.

Her dress is a tight, red rhythm section
barely holdin her flesh frae spillin
oot intae wild improvisations.

She dips, sways, her hips lead
while her breasts play independent harmonies.
She balances on drumstick heels

tappin a teeterin percussion
while strummin the snare o the bottle she holds
in counterpoint wi fuck red finger nails.

Aye, it's a catchy number alraight,
ah cannae help mahself frae swayin alang
tae the very same tune.

Ah raise mah glass an wi mah head
gae a cymbal crash towards the bar.
She nods an ah wet mah mouthpiece

an move tae join her, hopin mah tunin's raight,
that we'll be playin in the same key,
that ah can catch her every rhythm toneet.

Smooth Crocodiles
(for Jana)

Straight from the bar we creep,
giggling, to the half-buried beach ball
of Hotel Poseidon's heated pool.
Unzipping the huge flies that hold
the bulging polythene dome together
we step into steamy warmth.
We enter a hothouse, yellow light rippling
through clear waters, steam enwrapping us,
creating a mystery of the far walls,
lianas of steam twisting up dripping polythene.
We enter the innards of a tropical beast,
warm, gurgling, hissing, digesting us
in its slavering heat, swallowing us
out of the cool night outside.

We unwrap each other and glide naked
into the pool, smooth crocodiles
tumbling over and over, baring
our teeth, concealing them
with each others' lips and tongue,
feigning attacks, traversing the length
of our lake locked together,
our bodies strange and new
in this alien environment, freed
from gravity, convention, shame.
Condensation glistens, trickles
down the inner skin in a map of veins,
falls in cold drops to send
tremors quaking over the surface
making magnified flesh beneath
ripple in warm shivers.
Silver bubbles send quivering kisses
over our eager bodies.

We feed without blood, willing prey,
the penetration is soft
as a body sliding into water,
leaves without scar, enters again.
We kiss then kiss again.

Beneath the neon stars
love blossoms like a tropical flower.

The Morning After

We share a last cigarette,
formally thank one another,
pull on last night's battle-soiled uniforms
and leave in opposite directions
as soldiers might after a one day truce,
our minds moving in different languages.

Jacuzzi

It starts with a hiss, a rumble of indigestion,
then the rolling of distant thunder.
The surface seethes, a rainstorm puddle.
Bubbles tickle follicles, body hairs
like charmed snakes sway back and forth,
a nursery school of racing tadpoles ripple
over the whole body.

The force increases. Water leaps
like molten lava; cells dance,
peas in rapid-boiling water.
Tiny fists of air pummel limbs,
muscles relax, lesions freed
by the vigorous liquid massage.
The whole body is tossed like salad,
shaken by turbulence,
heads bounce along the pool side
and spurts of water leap so high
that eyes can only meet in glimpses.
Except for the blankly smiling faces
it seems a simmering cannibal goulash.

The pressure is turned up a little more.
The water is stampeding.
The storm is such whole bodies are raised,
lifted from the tub, then disappear grinning
beneath the waves.
Bony joints dislocate, body parts pop loose
like corks from over-shaken champagne, like
human Airfix models, construction processes reversed.
The Jacuzzi is a seething mess of
knee-caps, knuckles, ankles, toes,
a feeding frenzy in a shark banquet.

A tongue lolls over the side
like a wet chamois leather,
a pink slug trying to escape,
an elbow surfaces, the flash of a shark fin,
the hairy crab of a male left hand
cups the sea slug of a dismembered penis,
the skinless testes bob free,
smooth and shiny as sea-polished pebbles;
the buoyancy aids of a pair of breasts
rise inside the petrified
octopus grip of a unfleshed ribcage,
a little finger, curled and pink as a cooked prawn,
hooks into an ear's sea-horse spirals;
the closed up sea anemone
of a pinkly puckered anus
sinks beneath a coral pink
half-closed vaginal clam;
the sabres of single ribs glisten,
dart like barracuda,
around the coral crenulations
of a pulsing, floating brain
while intestines trail like medusa tentacles.

As the bubbles subside
the occupants start
to pull themselves together;
slot pearly teeth into
the mouth's shiny inner shell,
gather pale-mollusc finger-nails,
reassemble and leave,
shyly wrapping flesh in towels.
They will avoid each others' eyes
if they pass in the street tonight.

Trapeze

Hanging, curled below the perch –
sweet fruit, tantilisingly
beyond reach. Tendons tighten –
a slow melt into motion,
uncurling with the effortless
awakening of opening bud
unfurling to embrace sun's warmth;
a feline contorting
into spine stretching arc:
you become as moon –
a bright, calm, suspended crescent.

How do you hang so still
while my heart beats so fast?
How do you control such effortless poise
while I convulse with each measured turn?

The tightly reined tension,
the terror, the beauty,
but also the knuckled twist of guilt
for always the pleasure,
the joy, the fear,
is spiced by desire
to see you fall.

Tiptoeing up the Mountain

Gasping behind you up the knee turning incline,
cobbled with tufts, paved with cracked mud,
I am in awe of your graceful ascent.

Heels elevated you tiptoe up the hillside,
above you only clear air, sky,
each loose stone raising you toward the peak,
while I toil behind, flatfooted, breathless,
trying to stamp the mountain flat.

Fragile Cargo

I'm sorry I woke you - I heard the noise,
registered movement in the arid night,
never imagined to see so many bodies
flung like broken sugar cane,
some moving, some still,
never imagined such screaming and wailing
assaulting our great silver goldfish bowl bus
that floats on serene,
untouched, almost, by drama in action
through movie screen windows.

We cling to each other like monkeys in winter,
the video of my brain replaying
the distorted faces, heads cushioned in bloody hands,
the woman's body splayed, still,
shocked by our own dispassionate mortality.

Locked in the stinking cubicle
we link bodies, fuck blindly,
your face is wet, and mine,
hot and salty as blood,
but we continue the only way we know
with this fierce avowal of life -
with wet eyes and mouth we kiss
again and again and again.

Awakening

Last night when you confessed your dalliance
with my brother and your plans for alliance,
I must have looked like a desert dweller
whose always known of, but never quite be-
lieved in the idea of sea,
then woke one morning to set my eyes on …
nothing – all around – but blue horizon.

Skin Diving

Gulping deep breaths
you take me down to swim with you,
to explore the depths,
to analyse this world below

the surface; clawing through weed and stone,
disturbed at how incomprehensible,
how separate,
this world is from my own

I rise; we surface, I,
convulsing for air,
confused, disorientated,
unsure of what I find

in once familiar surroundings; you,
still wishing to dive below,
to lead me down,
to view this land we thought we knew

from angles that are hard to imagine.
I'm happier playing in the shallows,
too afraid of this sea's all encompassing grasp
to risk the reward of discovering pearls.

The Man Who Saw Too Much

It started without me really noticing.
I thought it the onset of summer,
a shedding of layers, a general replacement
of the heft of winter wool
with more diaphanous wrappings.

I became aware of the shapes beneath,
of how limbs slumbered under the clothing
as if filmed through thin cotton
with strong back lighting.
It was a gradual clarifying of vision,
not the slap of perception of new glasses
or wiping the mist from a window.

Soon I could see clean through the clothes,
the layers seemed to clear like smoke
and leave a cloudless view
to the bare hills and plains and valleys
of the naked bodies beneath.

Of course I made the most of it.
Searched out my crushes from adolescence
to watch the whole, unedited feature
having previously based my entire review
on only the briefest of trailers.

I couldn't get enough of flesh,
spent my days in constant arousal,
watched college girls walking,
cycling, running, laughing, sitting, smiling,
bounteous older ladies gardening,
their flesh hemmed in by corduroy
I could no longer see,
skin creased and folded beneath

like unironed laundry.
Any leading lady would
give their fan club to be able to film
themselves like this,
nude yet supported, scaffolded, propped, braced.

I watched men whose soft dough bellies
bore the imprint of each tight stretched button,
the stitches of their denim waistband
cutting seams into their abdomen,
cock and balls nestled like sleeping mice, new born.

But finally flesh lost its intrigue.
I began to look deeper.
Skin took on a translucent glow,
shimmered, flickered with the blood beneath it.
I stared at the twitching mesh of veins
stretched over pulsing, flexing muscle,
the network of nerves radiating
in quivering tendrils of grassy roots
over the rocky seams of bone,
the blood gushing in magma spurts
from the pulsing volcano heart.

I watched the car crash of growing clots,
the spreading vines of cancer take root,
the thickening of sluggish veins
the blotting paper leak of blood.

It scared me. I stopped going out.
What would they do
when the world found out?
I wrapped my head in wet towels,
having no sand to bury it beneath.
I ground lenses from the base of whiskey bottles,

shaped them with my teeth,
wrapped them in wire,
wore them as glasses,
never leave the house without them.

I pass others in booze bottle specs
looking down at the opaque tarmac.
We avoid each others' eyes,
we never speak, it's the safest way by far.
We do not like to be reminded
of all that we've learnt not to see.

Sgriob

On days so cold the woolly hanks
of passers' breath are left when they have gone,
snagged upon the barbs of frozen air,
and auguries of glazed puddles
lend a window
to the mottled bone and shadow
of an impending underworld,
and ghostly sheep led home for long nights
are lost between the mist of field
and their own breath's fog,
on a day such as this the Gaelic shepherds
coined a word unique to their tongue –
sgriob – a term rich in anticipation
to describe the itch upon the upper lip
in those delicious moments leading to
the inaugural sip of the water of life,
that first whiskey of the day.

Rendezvous

And he said,
'Let's take a walk on the beach,'

and she agreed that it was a good idea
and went to the loo to freshen up
and pull the ring from her second finger

and he finished up his half flat beer
and did the same with his finger collar,
glancing guiltily about the bar,

and so they walked, arm in arm, along the beach
until they came to a place where
the only litter was shells and pebbles
and charred wood washed up by the sea

and he said he was a sales director
and as a pastime collected crustaceans
and she lied too, said she painted landscapes
but thought she'd have a bash at surf,
and an ambitious wave stretched up and wet their feet
and feeling the suck of sand beneath her
she stared at the storm of swirling grains,
the cooly boiling rush of foam;

as it drew back to the sea she said,
'It's like walking on water',
and laughed because they were,
but not quite in the way that she'd meant

and there they kissed, and looking back
she saw their footmarks, looking like one creature's
so perfectly were their steps matched

and moving up to drier sand
she lowered her knickers, threw them aside,
and placed her rippled arse
upon the cellulite of dimpled sand,
and he shuffled from his trousers
and neither minded that both were middle aged
and overweight a little,
and soon the surf engulfed their gulps and
gasps of passion. So she

went back to her Hoover and husband,
and he to his kids and company car,
and even the imprint of their heaving bodies,
wallowing in half-lost lust,
was washed away by oblivious tide
and neither spoke of that night, ever,

though she felt sure she'd seen a scrap of
sandy cotton hanging from his blazer pocket,
and never said, but rather hoped
that it hadn't been his handkerchief.

Prometheus

You bastard. You lit a fire in me,
laid a tongue of flame against
the touch paper and blew hot breath
onto the pink jewel of an ember,
made me glow, ignited me,
dripped sweaty paraffin until long licks
of flame lapped along my limbs,
sent flickering fingers tickling up
the knots of muscle, sparking straw dry
kindling of nerve endings, setting
white driftwood lumps of spine alight,
tightening twists of sinew, curling
tight as twirls of smoke and spreading,
bursting uncontrolled, unquenchable
through my tinder body
until the conflagration burst
into a wild explosion
of fire and light and sound and smell.
Spent, I sank back into a smouldering slumber.

Now you'd give this fire
to any slut who smiles your way, you shit,
this precious prize is ours
and I will have no other tasting it.
You deserve to have your liver
daily torn through your stomach wall,
you deserve the chains that fix
you to this fossil heart of stone,
you deserve a harpy tearing
through your skin, your flesh, your breast,
to give this gift so freely
that once raised me to the gods.

Fogbound

She knows the city is still in reach,
that somewhere nearby the beacon of a street light shines
but for this moment she is lost.
She needs him to be the golden thread,
to lead her back to a world of cars and clamour
but when she looks into his frightened eyes she see
that one step from the path will lead her
onto wild moors, into a land
where the gap between man and beast
is as unclear as the thick air.

She wants him to make his arms into a boat
and carry her through this rising tide of panic
to safe, firm land, but he can't, or won't.
They are beyond the range of fog horns,
lifeboats or logic. Doubt takes hold.
The fog guides his limbs like marionettes' strings.
It leaks through every move he makes,
smoulders from his frightened mouth.

The lighthouse of a streetlamp.
At last they dock at home
but it's too late.
The fog has pushed damp fingers
into her lungs, seeped into her mind.
It has smudged the edges
of how she sees him and she knows
however tight he presses his dry fingers together
he cannot make a life for her
that will not leak.

Ocean

We finish and you sigh and gaze up into my eyes
with a slightly shocked expression
as though surprised to find me there. We stare
trying to reacquaint ourselves with the face so different
to the one that we'd been picturing and smile
because it saves us from speaking, then hug
because it saves us from looking
before rolling apart, separate and silent,
as neighbouring continents, golden in prophecy,
that once conquered lose their exotic appeal,
the wet patch an ocean between us.

Lifejacket

Something untouchable has changed
in the darkness of the room,
like the hush of rain edging in
or the clock's ticking suddenly ceasing.

We embrace as if we would
meld like putty into one,
closer than we ever were
through months pretending this could be love

held tight by the acceptance
there is nothing to keep us together
and tomorrow we will drift, alone.

I cling to you as if you were
the one unperished lifejacket
on this vast, empty ocean.

Mending
(After 'The Source', Jean Sprackland)

With an engineer's precision
he dismantles the silver casing,
lifts the tiny mirrors of overlapping scales,
unzips the seam to delve inside
and tinker with the quick machinery,
unwind the springs that make it tick
and fix the inner workings.

The mechanism's imprecise.
It spills red black over his slab.
There is no lever linked to fins' flash,
no pulley system to instil the tail's flick.

The slots and switches are so well hidden
he cannot click the inner workings back in place.
It leaks over his delicate instruments,
already reeking of failure.

Back to When the World Made Sense

Today is all wrong. The world is out of kilter.
Time will run backwards.

I will regurgitate glass after glass
of golden liquid, watch it sucked into hissing pumps
and stored, sealed in a cask, egg tight,
the glasses stacked and shiny and clean.
I will talk, at first to anyone who'll listen,
and several who'd rather not,
and then only to my friends,
in clearer and ever more lucid sentences.
Then I will leave the bar,
watch it recede to the end of the street,
and back into my home.

A chair will spin across the room
from where it rests on its side
and I'll catch it on my foot and right it,
and sit there, laying a meniscus of salty liquid
over the shiny brown varnish with my shirt sleeve,
before absorbing it into my body,
sucking it all greedily up
through the tiny ducts in my eyes.

You'll rush in, your head bent,
and I'll mend the dinner service.
With one magician's sweep of my hand
the shards will leap together and fuse
leaving not even the lines of maps,
and rise, amid somersaulting cutlery,
neatly landing like flying saucers.

I'll loudly take back accusations
and angry words, gulping them down

less and less loudly
until I'm eating mewling promises, pleading,
my brows furrowed into a shallow V
of incomprehension and terrible confusion.

I swallow all of it up
and it is gone from the world,
leaving me whole again,
as you calmly take back every reason
why I am unsuitable, glue my heart back together
with a thin smile and a nervous kiss,
then leave me taking cool wet potatoes from a pan,
wrapping them into their dry skins,
sealed, whole again, with a sharp steel blade.

You will back out into a world
where time runs in its usual manner
and everything still makes sense.

Ways of Undressing

Letting heavy cladding drop like a demolished tower block,
piled on the carpet, heavy with cement dust
in a volcanic mountain.

Swiftly shedding office clothing, hurling the funereal cloths
stinking of print runs and flat screens and Tippex,
over the back of the sofa.

Unpeeling the layers of exotic fruit,
careful not to bruise the tender, succulent flesh beneath,
fumbling eagerly with unfamiliar trappings.

Nothing had prepared you for this shuffling uncertainty,
clothes taken from you by strangers,
a green gown made from the paper that dries your hands

in public lavatories, and the journey to enforced dream,
to shining blade, unzipping skin to delve beneath.
The stitchings of flesh, another garment to be discarded.

Souvenir

"He should have better things to do at his age;
shelves to fix, pot plants to tend,
grandkids to think of and photos of his
mispent youth to fix in cellophane
and bore the neighbours' children with,

a fenced allotment in which to kneel
and make a daily worship of
with trowel and seed and sandy soil;

yet every day he ties himself
to this sagging chair
and stares at my half-opened window,
where I strip to shower behind lacy curtains,
pull on beach wear under blousy dress -
never quite revealing
more than the white tape of bikini line
holding golden thigh and torso together,
then step into shadow to dry the rest -
he never blinks, might as well be blind,
or dead for all that he reveals,
not knowing this voyeurism is a two way thing -
dirty bastard, he's never missed a single showing
all summer long,
yet never even caught as much
as is bared on the shop front posters,
advertising Lech and Zywiec beer
with sun on untanned cleavages -

you'd think he'd have a dog
to take for walks, things to do in a balmy summer -
Christ, what keeps the poor old fuck alive
through winter nights I wonder,
with guest houses empty, bodies clothed and beaches bare -"

And yet, with bags stuffed full,
trailing streamers of hair ties and bikini straps
(holiday bunting of bikini straps)
the last sand washed from under toe nails,
half dressed already for city life,
she stands, hooks thumbs under shoulder straps,
lifts and slides them to her waist,
steps out of slim white panties
and pulls the lacy curtains wide -
stands, poised as if sculpted, for thirty seconds
watching as his motionless face
slowly struggles
with something he can't comprehend;

forehead raises heavy eyebrows,
lips extend toward ruddy cheeks
in what could almost be a smile.

The taxi growls outside;
she dresses, takes her bags and goes,
leaving only an empty tube of lotion
and this souvenir
of a golden summer's golden body
for him to hold to the empty autumn window,
to gaze at in his mind's eye,
like old polaroids
of past loves, not quite fulfilled,
of summers' promises, never quite requited.

Building Babel

You always liked to use your hands
instead of talking, build an offering
to show the things you couldn't say.

As a child you demanded
the scaffolding of Baby's pen
while Baby circled, shook the bars, a shuffling JCB.

The play pen was a cupped hand around a flickering flame,
the protective chicken-wire about the swaying sapling
that you trained upwards, inch by careful inch.

Always the tower came tumbling down
before it reached the heights you'd planned
leaving no evidence but rubble for all of your toil.

An unsteadiness, a weakness in the wrist,
a hesitancy laying that final block,
no matter how you longed to blame

the howls and shrieks of circling fate
you could not escape the fear
that the fault was in yourself.

You'd look in bemusement at the debris,
wondering which bright cube
had given birth to the collapse.

And here you sit, a mug of tea unsteady on the sofa's arm,
groping uncertainly with trembling hands
across the scattered bricks of your marriage,

reaching for something to offer the ones you love,
for a painted block not yet pregnant with failure
with which to start again.

Punchbag

I used to join in even,
when Ma was launching into him,
thought he was weak, pathetic,
an empty shirt blown in the wind.

She'd be all smiles outside the flat
but inside it would all kick off.
It wasn't until later I saw
the strength there is to a punch bag,

a quiet courage to absorb
that anger thrown day after day
and hold it safe so none ricocheted
onto me or my sneering sisters.

It's only now I realise
that accepting the jags and jabs and jibes –
just as the need to inflict them –
was also a kind of love.

The Ice Storm

We pass the church and climbers' graveyard silently.
The mists thin to show dark peaks.
Stone walls and paths cut scars into the mountain's hide.

At first, only the tips are touched,
grasses bedecked with glittering jewels
in clusters of droplets, dangling
like diamante earrings.

We climb higher.
The ice grows in canine, layered teeth,
coating rocks like wet polar fur.

Every grass stem is a one-sided feather,
the edge serrated and sharp as a saw.

Beneath our feet the ground becomes treacherous.
Each plant is coated, disguised,
making thick, coral tendrils of the scraggy grass.
We are held in subaquatic silence,
Drowned by mist, colours submerged, sound muted.

The frosted ground, bone white,
the icy rocks glistening black,
a salt-print photo on a zinc plate,
a frozen image of an antique time.

The mountain's side looms unexpectedly,
shadow dark and sheer.
A stain of disturbed scree
points arrow-like to the cliff's roots.

We approach as swiftly as the terrain allows,
the air speckled with falling white

turning vision to static.
Head torches cut tunnels into thickening air.
The needle snow cuts into eyes.

When we reach him
the walker's body is almost covered,
has become tumuli,
a smaller shape held in his arms.

They look like they're sleeping.
Father and son, curled together,
broken leg splayed at an awkward angle.
An apostrophe; lives abbreviated by ice and wind.

The larger body lies wrapped round the smaller
in concentric snail shell curls.
The snow lies over them like a duvet.

We try to lift them. They are petrified.
Spittle, sweat, tears, blood,
the stuff of life turned to mountain stone.

For our ancestors Hell was always frozen;
only in more recent history,
beneath the desert sun of Gehenna[1],
has Hell become a conflagration.

We carry our burden to the village,
our hearts ruled by older gods.

---

1 *Gehenna* – a valley outside Jerusalem where Canaanaites once sacrificed children. The place became an area of abomination and was where the bodies of executed criminals and refuse were burnt. The first known images of Hell as a place of fire come from this.

How to Deliver a Baby

'Female Schindler' who saved 2,500 dies at 98. Irene Sendler, who was known as the 'female Schindler', rescued children and babies from the Warsaw ghetto in Poland, smuggling some out by wrapping them as parcels. May 13, 2008, The Metro

1. Make sure you have enough work space, then roll out the wrapping paper. Be sure you have enough paper to fit around the entire baby. Choose baby-wrapping paper that comes on a tube instead of pre-cut sheets of paper that come folded into squares. The latter have deep creases, which can give your baby a crumpled, untidy appearance. Measure if necessary, leaving a few extra inches to be sure your baby is completely covered.

2. Once the paper is cut to the right size, place your baby face down in the middle of the paper. Bring paper from the long side of the baby, up to the middle of your baby. Pull both sides tightly so the paper hugs your baby smoothly, and tape closed.

3. Next, you need to close the ends. Face the open end towards you and fold the right and left edges, pushing the sides in next to your baby, to form flaps.

4. Fold top flap down to the baby, pulling tightly, and tape. Fold the bottom flap up tightly and tape. Repeat on other side of baby.

5. Position baby so top is facing up. Run your thumb and forefinger across the edges of the baby to create a creased edge. Repeat on bottom of the baby.

6. To guarantee delivery, ensure sufficient postage is firmly stuck to the baby.

(Taken from ebay.co.uk/How-to-Wrap-a-Parcel-Gift – selected words replaced with 'baby')

Still Life

The blue flashing lights freeze the action
to a flickering old film, a linked series of still paintings.
The car is motionless. The steam rising into the cold air
is a wisp of cotton wool glued onto the black, sugar paper
night.

The driver is sitting on the pavement,
his face slumped open with shock.
It crumples over several frames,
like a sheet of tissue paper, screwed up.

He makes a mask of cupped hands as the small body is covered,
lifted onto the stretcher and slid through the white van doors
like childishly moulded clay into a kiln.
The flashing lights drain the scene of the palette of life.

Even the dark, wet pools on the road are blue-black,
like ink spilt across the school boy's desk.

The Naming

We lie like lovers in the dark, your arm
across my chest, my thigh against your thigh.
Your breath is warm, at last your breathing calm
and measured. I close my eyes and for a while
there is nothing else. No screams, no canons' thunder,
no, nor freezing mud, nor fear of death,
no enemy, no slipping slowly under,
no ragged hole in chest, no rattling breath.

I cannot find a name for this feeling,
lain here beside you in the wordless dark,
and do not want to, need no language stealing
in, for what cannot be seen or named can't mark.
We would lie safe if I could hold the words from forming
but daylight, in her treachery, will come, naming everything.

Defeating Gravity

Have I told you the tale of Icarus?
How he and his father stepped onto thin air and flew,
flew from captivity?
Imagine the feeling, an air cushion beneath your chest,
gliding onto winds warm and buoyant as the Med,
floating on a cloud lilo. The ending?

Don't worry about the ending.
Imagine the view, even better than from our perch
up here on the fourteenth floor.
Imagine the view as they soared above the turrets and towers,
the farm yards and factories.

I know it's hot, my love. Keep away from the door.
We'll press another towel along the crack.

I'll not think of dark tentacles
of smoke stretching into your lungs,
clinging to, smothering alveoli,
forcing their choking passage
down your protesting throat,
a boa constricting, a black wolf squatting
upon your chest, pinning you to the scorching floor
as orange tongues stretch up
to lick black strips from your bare arms and legs.

What if we were Daedelus and Icarus?
Striding from the broken window
into that ocean-wide blue
to float above the tower blocks and touch down
safely on some golden meadow?

Hold me, darling. Hold your daddy.
Be brave and take my hand.

Lost in the Forest

It could be a forest.

After a while
each tree looks the same
just as every anti-
septic wall, each pane
of glass, each strip-light does.
I cannot follow
the trail of crumbs back to how you were;
all have been swallowed
by greedy flocks, flapping in
on cancer black wings,
taking your strength,
your wit, your flesh – everything
that was you but this shell, cracking,
parched, unresponsive as gingerbread.
I know you are there, somewhere.
But part of me fears you've been misled,
kicked head-first in, the door slammed tight,
the dial turned to mark ten,
banging the heat-proof screen of that hot,
airless box you wait for release when
we can't find
even a crumb to guide us,
just fairy tales, photos in shades of gingerbread,
a garden of memory and loss.

It could be a forest.

The Greatest Circus in the World

It was the greatest circus in the world
but it paid a great price in the siege.
They were true to the city, as brave as our leader,
they gave their all for our great victory.

The bearded lady cheeks are soft as sponge cake
since she donated her whiskers
as blankets for our freezing soldiers,
the strongman is so worn down
from building the barricades single-handed
he can barely raise a half-pint glass
or guide his cripple-chair to the bar.

The minister and lord mayor,
before their roles were declared obsolete,
praised the patriotism of the last true mermaid
as she sacrificed herself for the good of all -
the circus master prayed to a still extant God to forgive them
as the hot oil sizzled for her final plunge.

They were the greatest circus in the world,
truly exceptional, individual,
they gave their talent and their best
to build the new regime,
used their differences to let us be equal.
How fortunate there are no more like them.

I don't give a fuck what you did on your gap year

All you talk of is politics,
missing the point as you
fumble and falter through concepts that alter
each time you engage with them,
sweeping comparisons thrown
without factual back-up to back up
the groaning emotional tomes of new terms
you've half-learned using words from the papers
your parents and lecturers read
over croissants and latte
to feed you chewed up into edible morsels
for you to regurgitate now,
as you irritate all who surround you,
especially me,

oh you're so fucking pious,
say 'leaders are liars,' like it's some great fact
that you've cracked on your own,
'In times of universal deceit,' on you drone,
'telling truth will be a revolutionary act,'
say, 'It's Marx who said that,'
so I make a crack about Groucho,
but you've never heard of him
too young and serious and thin,
'No, it's Karl, let the workers unite,
opium of the masses, and all of that shite,'

and you laugh, though I don't see what's funny,
and ask if I've got any 'shit' I can give you for free,
for you drink every day and use drugs to experience
the mind-set of Burroughs and Kerouak,
the highs and the hardships, open and free,
unconventional, see, and you've been far out East,

and yeah you know the world, and you never eat meat
or wear leather, 'It's murder, not clever or kind,' you cry
and berate me for not helping children
in Sudan or Iran or Wu Tan Clan, 'Huh?'
but you've never heard of them,
hate every band who has ever had air play
then you tell me I'm OK, and maybe you may
introduce me some day to a mate who you say
is a second rate DJ. Hoo-fucking-ray.

With a confident swagger you stagger,
take hold of my shoulder, lean over,
say: 'Power to the workers, Brother!'
Well, don't patronise me,
'cos you've not worked a day in your life
and one swipe of Papa's magic card
would solve all of your hardships,
your pot and your hols.
The quote's Orwell, not Marx,
and you can't take your beer,
and I don't give a fuck what you did on your gap year.

Symbology

That the place for human effluent
to be jettisoned into porcelain chutes
should be signified by the emblem
of a standing human seems odd.

This stance with arms stretched out
away from the action,
is not the posture most men adopt
to urinate, hands gun-slinger wide.

And unlike these signs,
ladies, I'm told,
prefer not to stand at all,
at least not with legs pressed together so tight.

Out of context the logo could well confuse,
yet as a symbol for our disposable age,
that the sign of a standing man and woman
should signify the detritus left behind

is fitting, as future races try
to make sense of our sullied earth
picking through the toxic waste
for a single remnant of worth.

Cows

They know the end is coming.
They carry the knowledge of violent destruction
welling up within huge, sad eyes.
It is not despair that makes them move that way,
one slow joint slotting into the next,
each step slumped like a dropped sack of manure.
It is not despair, it is acceptance.
Buddhas of the grasslands,
the sideways chomp is a meditation,
the lowing moan an incantation,
the universal om channelled through soft throats
held low to the ground.
They guide in the apocalyse,
Low, pendulous udders counting down,
laden with milk that none will drink.

Panamericana

Sprawling shanty towns of reeds
and corrugated iron,
mud swathed walls,
polythene wrapped, electricity
pylons pass overhead, buzzing
with news of another world
without ever stopping
to leave their messages.
Huge swathes of wasteland,
blooming with rubbish,
bright covers and wrappings,
dust and squabbling redfaced vultures.
A hand painted sign proclaims,
'WITCH - magic potions, spells -
I will make your lover come back to you!'
Wall sized wooden plaques claim,
'Cutting down your woods creates poverty',
as though leaving them
standing could create wealth.

Through Piura the cotton harvest is over.
Huge palls of smoke hedge the road,
ebony, neo-classical columns.
We rise to yellow cliffs,
strata in horizontal bookshelf layers,
imprinted with pink shadows
of wheeling seabirds.
On the road down to Mancora
the number of shrines and crosses
tell the story of every bend.

Painted signs of how to boil water
to prevent illness, diarrhoea,

littered scraps of plastic black sacks of sand
piled high to hold El Nino at bay,
disease littered villages with three-legged dogs
and sweet names like Aguas Dulces,
Arroyo Corazon,
and through it all the Panamericana,
a faded, fabled yellow brick road,
flowing on to a promised land
of huge fridges and cable TV,
the pull of its current so strong
it terrifies most into tranced stillness
and others drags with it,
so far they're never found again.

Reaping

The earth was rich and red as if blood were sown
and ploughed deep into the furrows.
From this angle clumps stood like besieged turrets,
or crumbling limbs reaching for the sun.

This morning we lowered him into earth's gloom
and I drove off at speed, things unsaid, long buried,
pressing over my head, soil dark, clay heavy.
Through the engine's sob, regrets bloomed.

My hand is open, upraised as if sowing
or begging, dust clings to bruised hillocks of flesh.
The headlight curved like a ripe gourd, growing
from torn wire, lies by knuckles of tyre tread.

When they cut me from the wreck they said the earth saved me;
the car half-buried, dirt wrapping me like a duvet.

Heritage

Walking fast, eager to get ahead
we pace over uneven ground,
heads down, backs bent.

We stride across the broken bones of walls
effortlessly stepping over boundaries
built high by our fathers.
We barely stumble on the stones,
rising like the fossilised spine of some dinosaur.

The ground we have trodden
is already but a vague recollection
though if we looked back we could, perhaps,
still find our bearings and so go forward.

We go on, stumbling. We keep our eyes down,
focus on what's beneath our feet,
biting back the rising panic.
We have thrown out the old maps
and with each step the light is a little dimmer.

De Umbras Idarum

Giordano Bruno was a Dominican friar and scholar. He espoused Copernicus' theories and went beyond them in identifying our sun as one of an infinite number of stars. He was banished from Italy and taught in Northern Europe until lured back by an Italian nobleman. He was arrested in Venice 1591, then taken to the Inquisition's jails in Rome where he was imprisoned. He was burnt at the stake for heresy in Rome's Square of the Flowers on February 16, 1600.

16 October 1589, Venice

Padre Bruno, I am a devoted admirer
of your teaching and your works,
'De Umbras Idarum' stormed by head
with shadows and doubts of my own mind's construction
yet the shadows were caused not by obstruction,
but by the fire lit by the sparks
of your thought, shining on my blunt beliefs,
honing them for further instruction.
I pray you are well in your distant exile
and can return to us who esteem your words
to inspire your eager disciples at home;
I request, could you clarify a recent discussion
on Copernicus? Your bravery to interpret his views
as literal, I applaud,
but in my edition the preface states clearly
this science is simply metaphor.

20 January 1590, Oxford

Signore Mocenigo, I am father to none,
the Dominican shroud I cast off with my creed;
the candle of faith casts little light,
it clarifies only the shadows of doubt,
yet in the candle of intellect
is born that which clarifies shadows of ideas,
time gives all and takes all away;
everything changes yet there perishes naught.
read again Copernicus, comprehend
the logic they try to conceal
behind incense and gospel and shallow bluff,
calling his universe 'metaphor'.
I curse the fool-priest that saved Nicolo's flesh
with his misguided, prefixed apology
for truth is worth more than flesh and sinew
and earthly suffering a small price to pay.

For my part, I left France for Oxford
where I was told the light of enquiry burns bright.
I was misled. They will not condone
that I lecture in their closeted university.
The feeble sun lights my way,
as unreachable to us as God, and I
will not hide in shadow, avert my gaze,
to save censure from those too scared to see.
The gates of enquiry are closed and locked,
and it seems in all Europe only I
can open their minds to the obvious truth,
yet they will not let me turn the key.
They bark and whine like Cerebus
at any questioning of the Greek pagan's lie;
the dead hand of Aristotle
still throttles reason's lonely cry.

The winter sunlight casts long, pale shadows,
like stains of something not yet formed,
intangible as ghosts –
the shadows of faith, or of ideas,
and our interpretation of season's turn,
I know, are all our own,
the sun changes not, the effect we observe
is our globe's rotation, inclined through the years,
yet stamps such an impression on our disposition
that on grey days like these, my thoughts turn to home
for my inspiration feels unbounded
when the vapours lift and the way is lit clear,
not shrouded in darkness. I complain unduly.
I knew long ago these climes are inclement,
'tis when faced by mentalities equally dulled
I lament for my motherland's warmer temperament.

10 June 1590, Venice

Egregio Bruno, I humbly entreat you

to share your knowledge, your worldly insight

and vision of this globe we inhabit.

Too long has your motherland made you an outcast,

return to her arms and teach her again:

I am not alone, I vow you will find

The climate improved, a renaissance of thought has arrived,

and even the Church cannot cast

out such clarity as in your manuscripts.

'De La Causa, Principio et Uno' has set alight my mind,

while 'The Ass of Cyllene' and 'The Art of Lully'

persuaded me that I must ask,

nay, implore, that you accept my request;

I am a man of considerable wealth, and privilege

and would learn from you all you have to teach,

should you accept my protection and patronage.

18 March 1591, Wittenberg

Signore Mocenigo, the angle
of the morning sun makes a tracery
of the sheep's paths across the hill's furrowed hide.
Spring. The shadows are shortening,
becoming denser, distilling, and the sun
through the first spears of leaf-bud flickering,
mottles the ground beneath where I sit
to write of my thoughts of returning.
My travels have left me in Germany
where I teach the few who will listen clearly
and the fewer who try to comprehend.
I am paid to translate, but my own work is suffering.
Your offer of patronage, a quiet retreat
to study and write in warmer climes appeals;
there is little clarity of thought here
and the patronage of kings is long gone from me.

This last week past I crossed the Elbe by boat;
the clouds broke and the golden sun
shone onto the waters, its glorious reflection
blinding us to the approaching shore.
I squinted through my cupped fingers,
focussing on the beauty to come
while my companions looked back
at the looming cloud behind, a dark and opaque pall.
Scripture teaches morals, not astronomy,
despite Lully's theo-scientific contortion.
Faith is contrary to philosophy,
which needs must set doubt upon all accepted laws
while Mother Church curls, porcupine tight,
her dogma a bristling phalanx of spears,
in this universe Copernicus charted,
the sun's angle beckons; I will return, without fear.

30 May 1591, Venice

Your Most Christian Majesty,
Head of the Holy Roman Empire and all its Legions,
I offer you, humbly, and as a sign
of my devout faith and devotion
Giordano Bruno, the infamous heretic,
his treachery not tempered by age or reason,
I enclose his correspondence as proof,
full of radical treatise and sharp subversion.
Send guards, well armed, to the address within,
lest he inflict injury to add to his treason
and let him stand trial, before God and The Church,
for his heretical perversion.
I trust this missive serves you well;
I enclose all details, compelling and pertinent,
and am, as ever, Signiore Mocenigo,
your faithful and devoted servant.

12 February 1600, Rome

Mocenigo, if that is your name,
you wrote as a scholar, not an enemy of thought,
I leave you a vision of the larger universe,
that expands in the infinite stars and mind
to combat the Ass of Cyllene, found everywhere,
in colleges, in courts of law,
in the Church which enforces ignorance
through the cowardly instinct to merely survive.
They condemn me to die, tied to a stake,
then ignited like a falling star
for my resolve in paths of the spheres:
they claim the truth of Copernicus and I:
"Erroneous in faith", "formally heretical",
"foolish and absurd in philosophy".
I do not contend their conclusions wrong in gospel,
but ungrounded in astronomy.

They trace the tracks of the sun's journey
throughout the daytime sky,
their knowledge based on blind conviction
and ancient scripture proving them right,
that we live at the universe's pivot;
they will not be convinced by fact or rhyme,
reason has no voice against centuries' prejudice,
science no commerce with Papal might.
My body they caged nine years in stone and dogma,
but cannot keep my thoughts confined:
in the Square of Flowers, in the centre of Rome,
they stack their sticks and prepare my pyre,
here at the universe's pivot, as flames transform
my flesh, as prayer proves me wrong,
the earth continues to spin
along its elliptical course around the sun.

Also Available from BeWrite Books:

Stick Figures
by Kirsten Holmes

Presented with Kirsten Holme's collection, Stick Figures, I beheld a persona equal parts fragility and hardness, the fragility being Kirsten Holmes' human vulnerability, the hardness being her exceptional ability to stand off, look with held open eyes at what has passed, and then to hammer out these, at times hard to read, poems. And they're diamond hard these poems, each dense with imagery, multi-faceted jewels. Get hold of them. Light up your mind.

paperback ISBN: 978-0-9866428-0-7
ebook ISBNs:
    EPUB: 978-0-9866428-2-1
    MOBI: 978-0-9866428-1-4
    PDF: 978-0-9866428-3-8

Heart with a Dirty Windshield
by Howie Good

"Howard Good turns words into a reciprocating saw that can be worked through your gut. He has internalised the existential horror of existence and turned it outward."
Nathan Tyree

"Howie Good's poetry sleeps with your wife and mocks you in front of your friends. It smokes your last cigarette and hides the remote before spending your grandmother's Social Security check on brightly menacing tattoos. Howie Good's poetry, the reader suspects, works for the Yakuza."
Jason Cook

"Howie Good's poetry remakes reality with startling images, disquieting insights and unexpected juxtapositions. The effect is by turn surreal, disconcerting and always compelling."
Juliet Wilson

paperback ISBN:978-1-906609-47-4
ebook ISBNs:978-1-906609-48-1

Peninsula
by Peter Loney

Peter Loney's 'Peninsula' is not so much poetry of place, more place as poetic lens. The place is Cumbria's southern peninsulas. Born in Barrow-in-Furness, Peter spent a lifetime teaching in Bosnia, lived in the US, worked for the World Service, and ended up in Ulverston. The lens takes in many of this life's experiences – the only poet Peter knew in Bosnia is now on trial in The Hague for war crimes – and tries to reconcile those experiences with a lifetime's reading.

Peninsula 9

In the Co-op earlier the tills broke down.
While staff tutted and fiddled I heard
Currency tumble by the hour, dishevelled
Girls at our Koševo checkouts break down,
Yoy! Yoy! Helpless to keep up
With the unhinging spiral. Quitting the shops
For the dewy tomb-choked churchyard
On the outskirts, the bench where I sit moored
In stagnant smaragdine light, snaps flooded back
From that pot-holed road-trip before we got out
And roads closed. Our visit to the Patriarchate
In Peć, Vesna uneasy as we looked
At the venerable mulberry-tree in the grounds,
Berries splattered red on the flagstones.

"Peninsula is ... ambitious, well-crafted, learned and wonderfully bleak." *Andy Croft*

paperback ISBN: 978-0-9877081-6-8
ebook ISBNs:
    EPUB: 978-0-9877081-7-5
    MOBI: 978-0-9877081-8-2
    PDF: 978-0-9877081-9-9

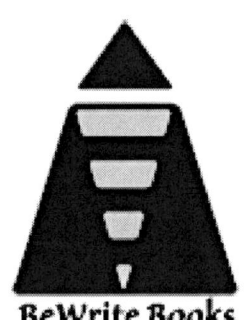

BeWrite Books

Lightning Source UK Ltd.
Milton Keynes UK
UKOW052226200412

191218UK00001B/1/P